INTER-SCHOOL SOCCER FINAL

CRASH!!!

WHACK!

SEE! TOLD YOU! ANOTHER PERFECT...

...LANDING.

OOOOoooooOOOooooo.

4

I KNOW IT'S SCARY TO BE TOLD THAT SOMEONE YOU LOVE HAS CANCER, BUT IT'S LESS SCARY ONCE YOU UNDERSTAND IT.

CANCER IS A TERM USED TO DESCRIBE *CELLS BEHAVING BADLY.*

IT'S WHEN CELLS DON'T ACT THE WAY THEY'RE SUPPOSED TO ACT.

ALL RIGHT, GANG, GRAB YOUR GEAR.

ANOTHER PERFECT LANDING!

SOMETIMES I AMAZE MYSELF!

YOU WANT ME TO CLIMB THAT THING!?!

ARE YOU COMING OR WHAT?

GO ON WITHOUT ME...

8

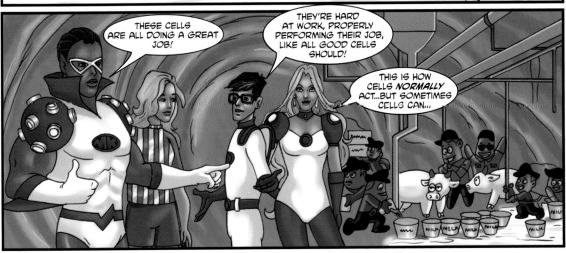

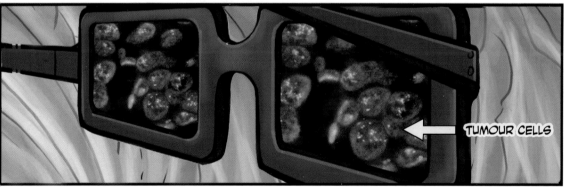

COOL! HOW DOES IT WORK?

IT ONLY KILLS CELLS THAT GROW *REALLY FAST.*

THIS MEANS IT KILLS BOTH THE *CANCER* CELLS AND SOME OF THE *NORMAL* CELLS THAT GROW QUICKLY.

LIKE *HAIR* CELLS...

MAKING YOUR MUM'S HAIR FALL OUT.

YOUR *BLOOD* CELLS...

MAKING YOUR MUM FEEL TIRED.

AND *STOMACH* CELLS...

MAKING YOUR MUM FEEL SICK.

WILL SHE EVER FEEL BETTER?

THE SIDE EFFECTS USUALLY STOP ONCE THE TREATMENT STOPS.

OH, GOOD.

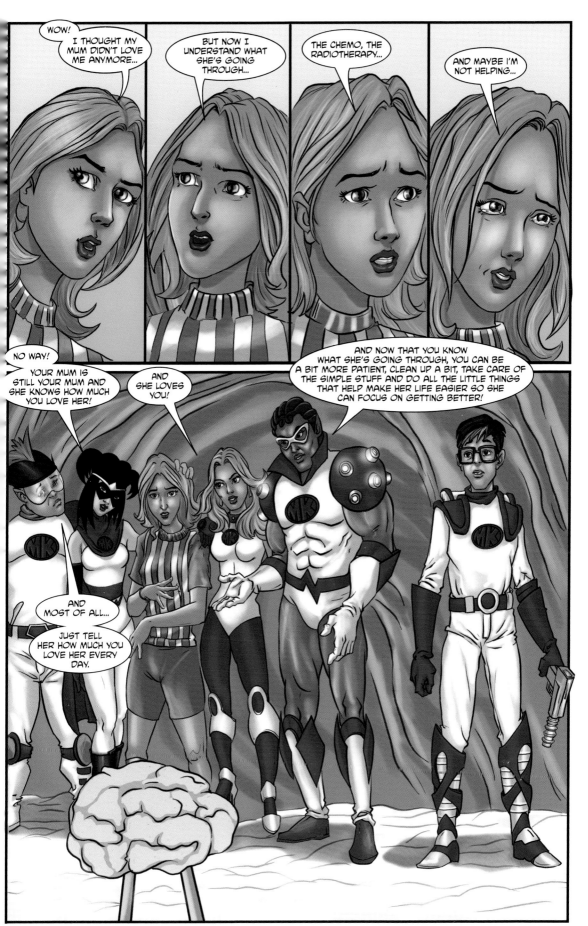

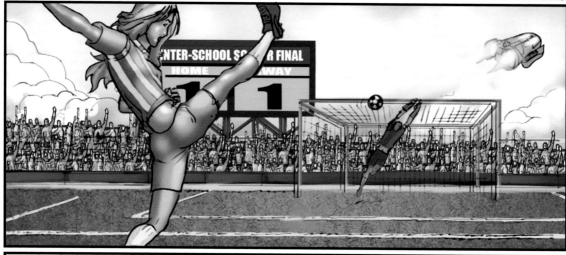

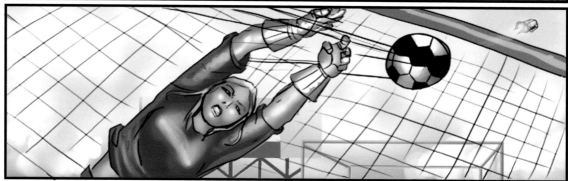

29

WHOSE A+ AND CHAMPIONSHIP TROPHY IS THIS?!?!

MUM!